The Little

The Little

A to Z

A Companion for

FIRST-TIME MOTHERS & THEIR PARTNERS

Rachel Perks, PhD

SHE WRITES PRESS

Published 2020
Printed in the United States of America
ISBN: 978-1-63152-681-7
ISBN: 978-1-63152-682-4
Library of Congress Control Number: 2019920932

For information, address:
She Writes Press
1569 Solano Ave #546
Berkeley, CA 94707

Interior design by Tabitha Lahr

She Writes Press is a division of SparkPoint Studio, LLC.

To all new parents seeking to raise their little ones
from a place of humility, patience, and love.

To my co-parent and partner, without whom this
great journey would not be possible.

FOREWORD

When I had my baby, I was a stranger in a foreign land in more ways than one.

I was new to the art of motherhood. My girlfriends who had children were scattered—on the West Coast of the United States (US), and in the United Kingdom (UK), Kenya and Canada, and Myanmar. Of my friends in the District of Columbia (DC), only one had children. My parents lived thousands of miles north, across the border in Canada. For all intents and purposes, I was without a baby community.

Beyond this, I was a stranger to the culture of child-rearing in a developed economy. For over a decade of my professional life, I had witnessed children being raised in some of the most difficult terrains in sub-Saharan Africa. I had also witnessed children growing up in the most luxurious households in these same regions. I didn't have to worry about boiling water for bathing my son; I didn't have to wash diapers by hand. But I also didn't have the nannies, housekeepers, and drivers that many of my friends living abroad had to keep our household ticking along. The contrasts between the experiences I'd witnessed came back to me time and time again in the first months after my child was born.

Most importantly, I was a foreigner living in the United States. I didn't know what to make of the obsession with "stuff" for babies—perfect diaper bags with monograms on them, or perfect strollers that met all the safety regulations—and the pressure to do baby showers and registries. It was all too much—and not me.

So much time is spent preparing expectant mothers for the actual birth, but there's little attention given to the aftermath, which goes on for much longer! There were so many things that my husband and I didn't know. I often found myself wishing for a small reference book that I could open quickly, an A to Z guide to motherhood at my fingertips. I imagined its pages, worn from frequent use. A vision of this little book kept coming back to me throughout those first months. I'd had one before: *Bush-Friendly Tips for Girls (and Boys Too!): The Ultimate Guide to Safari in Kenya*. It was witty, and illustrative of the female capacity to find humor in very serious "bush stuff."

Perhaps others yearned for a "parenting how-to" guide like I did. Perhaps others felt as lost at times as I did. Being the good PhD student I had been, I started doing my literature review. I got books out of the library about motherhood. I looked at best sellers. I laughed, I cried, I cursed myself that I had not found these treasures earlier. But many of them were priceless memoirs that I could not have fully absorbed at the time. In those busy first months, I wasn't looking for reassurance that it was all going to be okay. Instead, I was looking for someone to tell me how to make it okay *right now*.

That was the inspiration behind this little book: to create a small companion for parents to carry with them during those difficult first months. In it, I've weeded out a lot of the endless Google searches and offered some of my most meaningful finds and solutions. While researching, I shared ideas with friends—those who had more babies and more experience than me—and the *A to Z* grew, snowballing as responses came in from other mothers and fathers.

The following pages are the product of my wisdom and theirs—a collective voice across borders, time zones, and cultures.

That is, until you read it and add to where we have missed out (and I hope you will, in the blank pages left at the end of each alphabet letter's section).

Happy mothering!

A

is for . . .

A&D Ointment: Although the directions recommend using it when your baby has diaper rash, we ended up using it on a continuous basis after every diaper change.

Adaptable: According to the University of Kent, in this fast-paced, changing world of work, adaptability is one of the top ten skills employers seek in new recruits. Hello, new parents: Raising a little one is the hardest job you will ever sign up for. If the corporate world thinks adaptation is key to success, why not for our success as parents? The difference here is that unlike your job—where, to a certain degree, you can control the pace and your response to change—your role as a parent is shaped by a small human being who is rapidly changing, often with little warning.

I was most frustrated by how quickly the needs of our son, Clyde, changed in the beginning and how frequently I had to adapt my newly mastered routine. One day I was breastfeeding 'round the clock and my body had finally adjusted to the loss of sleep; the next day, he was sleeping through the night. Or one day he was napping twice a day, and the next, just once daily.

If you go back to work, being adaptable is doubly important and equally challenging, as you are creating two new routines: one for your public life and one for your private life. Even after two years, our routine still changes significantly. There is always something new cropping up—day care, later bedtimes, or new travel requirements. Success for you, your partner, and your little one will hinge on your collective ability to flexibly respond to the minuscule changes while still maintaining the foundations of daily routine and rituals essential for successful child development. This requires considerable communication between parents and sensitivity to the needs of your little one.

Once you let go of the illusion that you are in control, your ability to adapt will increase significantly. In fact, you may even start to enjoy the ebb and flow afforded by your child's daily routine of self-discovery.

Air (see also Outside): Getting out and breathing fresh air is restorative for you and your baby. This was evident to us early on in parenthood. Whenever my husband or I took Clyde outside, he slept better afterward. This included everything from laying him on the dog bed on the porch (with a sheet between him and the bed) to walking him in the stroller during those terrible witching hours to strapping him in a carrier and heading for the fields or trails. Now that he is past one year and much more mobile, his attention is caught by the smallest things outside.

Outdoor time has been good for me too. Now I notice buds on tree branches, shoots of grass, tiny flowers in the undergrowth, canopies of trees. I'm seeing the world through a new lens.

Apps: In the early days of breastfeeding, I found some specific apps very useful. One in particular allowed me to record the number of times I was feeding in a day and for what length of time. I used Sprout (although there are plenty out there). In the beginning, when everything felt overwhelming and I was running on little sleep, it helped immensely to record all of Clyde's feedings and bowel movements. Once I had established a rhythm and, more importantly, confidence in caring for my baby, I stopped using it.

Attention: The parent-child bond is created by spending time interacting with your baby. For mothers who breastfeed, establishing that connection is not so difficult. But as your little one grows out of breastfeeding, you will need to maintain that daily connection through other forms of interaction—physical touch and play, eye contact, story time, etc. Sometimes I caught myself with my mind a million miles away when I was with my son, or found myself multitasking—tackling chores, searching something on the Internet, or doing some other household task—while I was spending time with him. When you're with your child, be as present as possible. Give them your full attention. I make a conscious effort to put my phone and computer away and set aside distraction-free moments with Clyde on a daily basis.

B

is for . . .

Baby Highs: This refers to the feeling of elation and well-being that most mothers feel in the first seventy-two hours after giving birth. In my case, it lasted a bit longer than seventy-two hours. I recall Clyde sleeping in a sling on my lap as I worked on a paper I was submitting to an academic journal. I did a few days of marathon writing and feeding with very little sleep, then crashed (see *Baby Lows*).

Baby Lows: This refers to the feeling of "bottoming out" following those first seventy-two hours of baby highs. Most likely your hormones are fluctuating wildly at this point; also, the body is recuperating from a major physical, mental, and emotional undertaking, and it's running low on energy. For these reasons, it is good to be mindful of sleeping, resting, drinking lots of water, and eating healthy during this time. It was in this period of baby lows that I got mastitis (see *Mastitis*).

Bathtime (*see also* Nighttime Routine): It really is so much fun! We found a Fisher-Price whale bathtub for babies at our secondhand store. We brought it home, washed it out, and have been using it ever since (our son is now over two years old). It has a sloped back with a grip that allowed me to comfortably put Clyde in upright in those first months. I recall the first time he realized he could kick his legs around and make the water splash. It kept him entertained for a good fifteen minutes. What a great way to tire him out before bed!

Blackout Curtains: Newborns and babies need darkness to sleep—the darker, the better! They are easily distracted if their room has any kind of light in it. We rigged a pair of blackout curtains up over the regular window shades in our son's room. They are still there to this day.

Books (*see also* Literacy): Don't underestimate how early you can start introducing books to your child. My phone's screen saver is still a photo from when my son was seven months old, sitting on the floor and holding one of his books in his lap. Children's books stimulate the senses and the brain with pictures, colors, touch and feel, and sounds. In Washington, the District government mails a library of books to your home to get you kick-started. There is no need to register. We were so fortunate in this regard. In addition, for our baby shower we asked all our friends to give our baby their favorite childhood book. Before he was even out of the womb, he had the most amazing library! Some of our all-time favorites: *Harry the Dirty Dog*, by Gene Zion; *Goodnight Moon*, by Margaret Wise Brown; *On the Night You Were Born*, by Nancy Tillman; *Good Morning, Canada* and *Goodnight, Canada*, by Andrea Lynn Beck; *Dear Zoo*, by Rod Campbell; and *Good Night, Gorilla*, by Peggy Rathmann.

Boppy Tummy Time Pillow: Not many products deserve a plug, but this one sure does. We were given this pillow as a gift, and it was a daily companion from my son's second month until his sixth. This pillow is not the one for breastfeeding (that's another product of theirs). You can lay your baby in the tummy time pillow and eventually use it for tummy time and for helping your baby to learn how to sit up.

Bottle: Choosing the right bottle is another one of those agonizing tasks (see *Diapers*). We followed the lead of our lactation consultant and chose Dr. Brown's. The design claims to reduce gas, and we didn't have problems with that when we started using the bottles (you will still need to burp your baby). Cleaning bottles after every use is tedious but extremely important. I bought a large Munchkin bottle brush that helped get into all the crevices. And one of our friends lent us her Boon Grass countertop bottle drying rack, which was super helpful.

Breastfeeding (*see also* Lactation Consultant, Mastitis, Pumping): Breastfeeding is probably the most complex issue a new mother grapples with, because breastfeeding is not just about feeding—it is about women's rights and family rights, and increasingly it is about work-life balance, co-parenting, and careers. It is amazing to me that something so private is one of the most hotly debated public policy issues.

In our part of the United States, the emphasis is on breastfeeding. Significant public health resources are devoted to its promotion. Pediatric guidelines suggest we should breastfeed, if we can, for at least the child's first year. Yet almost all women have moments when they wonder whether to continue (if they breastfeed at all). It can be extremely challenging for a mother to physically breastfeed, and considerable emotions are attached to whether you breastfeed and for how long.

An important factor influencing a woman's choice to breastfeed is the lack of federally mandated paid parental leave. Many American households cannot afford for one parent to take leave without pay to stay home with a newborn. Once parents have exhausted leave options (paid parental, annual, or sick leave), women return to work. And when they do, they face a significant decision: will they continue to breastfeed? If women resume work and continue breastfeeding, then they must pump at work (see *Pumping*).

Once you navigate breastfeeding and work, you might face other emotional issues. In my case, I continued breastfeeding when I returned to work after six months of leave, but by month eleven, my supply was drying up. I felt enormously guilty when I switched to formula for my son's last month (after twelve months, babies can have cow's milk if they don't have allergies). I told myself, "I am no longer capable of giving him all he needs."

Every family must be comfortable with their feeding choice, but it would be nice for families in the US if they didn't have to make really tough choices that parents in almost every other country in the world simply don't face because they have paid parental leave (see *Maternity Leave*).

Breathing (*see also* Quiet, Self-Care, You): Mindfulness, meditation, or yoga can set you up with a solid foundation prior to childbirth. Breathing resets the mind and brings clarity to a situation. Feeling overwhelmed? Take a moment for yourself and do some deep breathing. You can sit in a chair, on the couch, on the floor, or even lie in bed. A few minutes are all you need to declutter the mind. One free app I absolutely love is Insight Timer. It has thousands of guided meditations to follow, or simply use the timer to practice some deep breathing.

Brest Friend: This pillow for breastfeeding could well become your best friend in those early months of motherhood. Originally, I had a different support pillow for breastfeeding and was having back pain. After seeing my lactation consultant, I got this one; it made a world of difference for my posture, and that eased my neck and shoulder pain. Definitely worth the investment.

Burping: There are so many ways to burp your baby after feeds. My favorite was over the shoulder. I'd take one of the gazillion burping cloths we were given, put it on my shoulder, and then rest my little one up on it. My husband's favorite was over the knee. We have some great photos of our son hunched over his knee. I'd say Clyde burped or spit something up only about 60 percent of the time. But it's still useful to dispel air in the system to prevent gas, even if you don't hear the baby burp or see some small amount of milk come out.

C

is for . . .

Carriers: If you are a walker, hiker, or frequent traveler, invest in one! You won't regret it. We went through two before settling on the one that we still use today. The heat and humidity of Washington, DC, and Virginia required us to find one that had some ventilation, and we ended up choosing the Ergobaby Adapt Cool Air Mesh. The few times I had to travel by air alone with our baby, I used the carrier to move in airports instead of lugging around a stroller. Much easier to get through the security scanners.

Classes: We put our son in some play classes when he turned six months old. We did a music class and a play group class. Both allowed him to interact with other kids. The location where we enrolled him in these early classes has now become his preschool, so he has acclimatized easily to the school, gradually going from being there one hour, to two hours, to nine hours a week. In our case, this was pure luck, but if you can think a bit ahead, try to find a school that can facilitate a slow transition for your baby. We believe it's made a big difference in Clyde's ability to transition into day care. It also gave us the opportunity to test out a day care at a very early stage without financially investing too much.

Co-parenting: In this day and age, most couples remain engaged professionally outside the home while raising kids, so co-parenting is essential for achieving work-life balance and positive relationships. Whenever my husband is changing a poopy diaper (which is often), he jokingly yells out from our son's bedroom, "Co-parenting!" But in all seriousness, it is the only way a couple will survive the intensity of modern parenting if both choose to work.

Just because co-parenting is essential to survival doesn't mean it's intuitive. There are a lot of gender norms that creep into even the most modern couples' homes. Reflexively, we adopt our parents' parenting model when we become parents ourselves. What to do when those models don't work for you and your partner?

Successful co-parenting requires foresight, planning, and sitting down often to review and revise what is and is not working. My husband is a pilot, and my work requires overseas travel. We continuously revisit the division of labor in our household, depending on who is facing the greater professional demands in a given week. It took a lot of discussion for us, coupled with trial and error, to get it semi-right. We don't have a rigid schedule that lays out who does what every day. But we do consider each other's workloads and responsibilities—both within and outside the home—and determine who can take on what as a result.

One important lesson I've learned is to not assume. Don't assume your partner intuitively knows that you want someone else to do the dishes, or book the holiday flights, or call the pediatrician. You must ask, and you shouldn't feel like you are weak when you do (see *Help* for a related discussion). Another important lesson I've learned is not to treat co-parenting in a piecemeal fashion. Meaning, avoid fighting one week over who will do the dishes, and then the next over who will do the early-morning wake-up. The best way—which we didn't do well in the beginning—is to look as holistically as possible at daily routines and personal needs and work through them in their entirety. It may seem overwhelming, but it will help you avoid feeling like you are haranguing your partner over "yet one more thing" every week.

Co-sleeping: I have plenty of friends who have co-slept with their children, some until at least five years old. There are a lot of advantages for the baby and the mother, including the ease with which one can breastfeed in those grueling first few weeks. We did some research on the subject and in the end decided not to co-sleep or to have our baby's bassinet in our room. I am a light sleeper and was concerned that with my infant in the room, I would never sleep properly. But my girlfriends who did co-sleep absolutely adored it, and they believe their bond with their child is that much stronger because of it.

Colic: My husband was a colicky baby, so we prepared for the worst with Clyde. To our relief, however, he never developed colic. My understanding is that it is a baffling combination of behaviors where your baby will cry and your efforts to soothe him/her won't help. This is, apparently, what makes it so frustrating. Pediatricians use the "rule of three" to diagnose colic: your baby must cry for at least three hours at a time, at least three times per week, for at least three weeks. In talking with friends who had colicky babies for periods of up to nine months straight, the best solutions seemed to be driving in the car late at night to get the baby to fall asleep and putting the baby safely in a bassinet or a car seat on top of the dryer and letting it run for thirty minutes or more.

Combat-Ready Balm: Another miracle diaper rash cream. This one is fancier and more expensive than A&D but is worth it if you like your baby's bum smelling like lavender.

Community: In a podcast interview, Sheila Pai discusses the impetus behind her concept of a "living community" and why it is so vital to create one after childbirth. Her "living community" is a response to the lack of nearby family (parents and grandparents) that many people of our generation are experiencing, as we have moved away from home in search of education and jobs.

Finding oneself without an immediate support network can be extremely trying in those early months of child-rearing. Intense feelings of isolation and helplessness are common. You need to have people around with whom you feel comfortable enough to be vulnerable and whom you are willing to ask for help.

I didn't have that nearby. I had dear friends who lived about an hour away, and most of them worked demanding full-time jobs. Not surprisingly, I missed my parents a lot in those first months. They know me inside out, so when I was overtired and overwhelmed, I knew I could be myself, completely and utterly, without worrying what they would think. I could ask them to take the baby so I could sleep, or to cook and clean for me. I might muster up the courage to ask a neighbor or a friend for this kind of help once or twice, but I could ask my parents repeatedly, without hesitation.

Sometimes I was simply overwhelmed by the effort it would take to ask someone for help. Other times I was afraid that someone might decline if I asked (which did happen sometimes!). In this sense, having my parents around would have been so much easier. I was grateful for my "living community" from the city, friends who graciously drove out to visit (some on a weekly basis) to deliver food and to help with shopping.

Constipation: This is a definite concern (for both you and your baby). In the hospital after delivery, we were given a chart by the pediatrician to log our baby's bowel movements, including color and texture. And when you do those first weeks of pediatrician checkups, a big topic of conversation will be your baby's bowel movements. I used the Sprout app (see *Apps*) to log them until I was comfortable that he was pooping regularly. For mommies, too, constipation is a concern, particularly if you developed hemorrhoids during delivery. You will want to remain regular to avoid any exertion when having bowel movements (see *Hemorrhoids*).

Cradle Cap: This is completely normal! As I write, our son still has remnants of his (little spots that remind us of those early days). If it bothers you, you can remove it with some shampoo and by running a small comb through the scalp. One of my girlfriends swore by the Australian brand Moogoo, which has a specific product to help with the removal of cradle cap if your wee one's head is quite covered with it.

Croup: This is a relatively common viral infection in babies and younger children. You'll recognize it if your baby develops a "barky cough." Our son had it once in his first year. The sound is alarming, but it went away fairly quickly. Mild forms of croup can be treated at home with lots of rest, a bit of acetaminophen (if they have a fever), and a humidifier to keep the air moist.

D

is for . . .

Day Care: If possible, it is advisable to keep your little one out of day care until they are one year old to help them build their immunity in those early months. But at some point, day care may be required. Where we live, facilities abound, and what we found most important were the following: 1) a facility that is within walking/driving distance of your home and/or your commuting route (if you work); 2) a curriculum that shares your values; and 3) a facility that privileges outdoor time. We started out with only a few mornings a week to build Clyde's routine there (see *Classes*) and provide him with a chance to interact with other kids before enrolling him full-time after the age of two. Over time, day cares might also be the place where you cultivate friendships with other parents in your children's classes.

Developmental Milestones: Some pediatricians' offices will provide you with a checklist of signs you can monitor in between prescribed regular checkups. Our pediatrician's office was very good about monitoring these signs during our visits and going through the list with us before sending us on our way. This is why it is so critical to go to your pediatrician appointments (see *Regular Checkups*). If you don't have that resource from your doctor, you can look the checklists up on the American Academy of Pediatrics website.

Diapers: How to choose? This is one area where my husband excelled at the decision-making. He researched various brands and did a cost-per-diaper analysis, and then we tested two major brands for "performance." We have been super happy with Target diapers. The quality is very good, there are no baby powder smells, and often Target has specials that allow you to buy several boxes and get a discount. But beware: someone has to monitor the usage levels. In the beginning, we went crazy purchasing diapers, forgetting that we had tucked some away in closets and drawers. Our baby grew so fast that we were on to the next size without having finished our supplies of the first. Don't be overzealous in buying! On some websites, like Amazon, you can place a monthly purchase order and get regular deliveries to your door.

Diaper Rash: Ouch, Mommy! Diaper rash comes in all shapes and sizes. It is tricky to monitor, as it can be brought on by small changes in the climate or because of food. Your baby is more likely to start experiencing it once s/he starts to eat solid foods. We live in a climate that is hot and humid in the summer, and we found that our son tended to develop diaper rash more easily then. You'll most likely play around with a variety of treatments until you find a few that work for the severity of the rash. For mild forms—red, irritated skin in very localized areas of the bum and small red bumps—we used a combination of A&D (see *A&D Ointment*) and baby powder during the day, and then applied Penaten (see *Penaten*) in the evening after a bath. For severe forms—red, irritated skin all over the bum with bumps that had little white heads—we'd either use Penaten continuously or apply an over-the-counter mild foot fungus cream, as recommended by our pediatrician. The most important thing is to keep the area clean: frequently check the diaper to make sure your baby hasn't pooped, and bathe him/her every night during the rash period. I found that baby wipes aggravated the rash even further, so I used a warm, damp face cloth to clean his bum during the diaper change instead.

Drawers: These are your best friend when traveling and you don't want to lug around a travel crib or playpen. We took several trips during the first six months, and our baby slept in a dresser drawer that we placed in the bathtub of a hotel room. It's pretty simple to engineer: You need a few towels for padding the drawer. Let them hang over the edge of the sides. Wrap a bungee cord around the sides to keep the towels in place. Voila! Stick the drawer in the bathtub and place the baby in the drawer on his/her back to sleep at night. Bathrooms are great because typically they are windowless, so they're very dark.

We did a road trip down from Maine through Vermont, New York, and Pennsylvania when Clyde was five months old, and this drawer trick worked like a charm. It also worked well when we stuck the drawer in the middle of beds in friends' houses and in hotels, or even on floors on a trip through the Rocky Mountains when Clyde was four months old.

Drinking: Cultural attitudes about drinking while pregnant and breastfeeding differ, from "absolutely none" to "occasionally a drink" to "a glass of wine every night." Different segments of society throw all sorts of proscriptions (and glances) your way. It's important to read the literature on the subject, and to read widely, including sites from outside of the US. In the end, you must do what you feel comfortable with.

E

is for . . .

Eating (Solids): Pediatricians in the US recommend introducing solid foods to your baby before they are six months old. Often, the first food suggested is rice cereal, but as my lactation consultant pointed out, rice cereal has absolutely no nutritional value. We skipped this and went with oatmeal. Remember, in the first months of introducing solids, all you are doing is giving your child a spoonful of food here and there. The transition off of breast milk or formula is still a long way off.

Before introducing these breakfast items, I read two books that shaped my approach to feeding my baby: *First Bite*, by Bee Wilson, and *Stress-Free Feeding*, by Lucy Cooke and Laura Webber. *First Bite* is a history of food and our relationship to eating over the ages. *Stress-Free Feeding* is a practical guide. I found the two books complemented each other very well, and both were evidence-based and well researched.

The first book brought one clear message home to me: as a species, we favor sugary foods. So, to reduce your child's chances of developing diabetes and obesity (remember, this is the US), you should introduce bitter vegetables to their diet first. I steamed kale, pureed it in the blender, and served it to our baby with my hands. What a mess! He rejected it. That's where the second book comes in. It says that your baby may reject a food up to twenty times before actually liking it. You just have to stick with it. Mix it up by offering five different vegetables with varying degrees of sweetness over the course of two weeks. You can play around with texture. Allow your child to grab with his/her hands.

In our case, within a few months we had a healthy eater who didn't turn his nose up at a single food.

Estate Planning (see also Guardianship/Godparents): This may be a difficult task to undertake since estate planning inevitably involves thinking about death or life-threatening disability. It is important to do, however, especially, if like us, you are a mixed-nationality couple. (I am not an American citizen.) My husband and I had no estate plan at our child's birth, and we only got around to it after our son turned two. We had at least selected godparents within a few months of our son's birth, which resolved the guardianship issue in case of death or life-threatening disability. But the broader task of wills did not come until later.

Expectations (see also **Adaptable, Flexwork,** *and* **Judgment**)**:** Some of us enter parenthood with a clear idea of what we expect from ourselves and our partners. Others do not. I found it important to manage my own self-expectations carefully, remembering that any ideas I had about how I was going to be as a mother were subject to change, and that this was okay. My first experience of confronting self-expectations was revisiting the idea that I would be a full-time career mother. Prior to giving birth, I had not even considered the possibility of working a reduced work schedule after my maternity leave. I had gone as far as to register our son for day care as soon as we knew we were pregnant. But one month before returning to work, I had this awful, recurring feeling at the prospect of returning to work full-time. I wanted to be a great worker, but more so, I wanted to be an excellent mother. The biggest challenge was to not feel guilt or shame that I was reevaluating my expectations for myself; then it was to vocalize this to my husband; and, finally, to talk with my boss about a new reentry plan.

One of my dear girlfriends shared her own perspective on the expectations we place on children. It's good to be realistic, she said, "but do your best not to place your own wants onto your children. Remember they're individuals and they need to figure out who they are. The only expectations I have [of my children] is to be polite, thoughtful, and always show kindness to others. Beyond that, I try to let them be and have no expectations—unconditional love!"

I couldn't have said it better myself.

F

is for ...

Fifteen Minutes: Many writers commit to spending at least fifteen minutes a day on their craft. Even though you might find yourself overwhelmed, taking just fifteen minutes a day to write can be useful. You'd be surprised at the emotional clutter you can clear. While I was on maternity leave, I journaled for fifteen minutes a day. It helped me to process a ton of very big, new, confusing, and overwhelming emotions. It allowed my mind to take a few moments away from the day-to-day. It also helped me remember the many little changes our baby was going through. The process of daily writing allowed me to savor the tiny, beautiful experiences I was having with my son on a daily basis.

Financial Planning: Money is a leading cause of marital stress, and doing some planning in advance of having children can ease the tension. Beyond thinking of a baby fund (see *Fund*), my husband and I didn't get very organized on the financial planning front. It was only about a year into parenthood that I came across this amazing podcast from the ThirdPath Institute that put things in perspective for me. Matt Becker, founder of Mom and Dad Money, shares his financial planning strategies for new parents in this particular episode of ThirdPath's monthly podcast.

Flexwork: If you are a millennial, you can skip this entry, as with companies seeking to retain talent, work flexibility is pretty much a given nowadays. If you are a Gen-Xer (like me), however, you will relate to the fact that some of the ideas on work-life balance were starting to creep into office and public debate when we began our careers, but certainly not to the same extent as today. In essence, flexwork is a human resource tool made available to employees to help them better balance and manage responsibilities within and outside the home. I encourage new parents to research flexwork options, perhaps even prior to becoming pregnant. In more traditional institutions like my own, the tool is more readily offered to new parents, particularly mothers.

I had thought that after my maternity leave I would return to work full-time. But as my maternity leave came to an end, I didn't want to leave my baby at home with a nanny all day, nor did I want to send him to full-time day care. So I read my institution's flexwork policies, talked it over with my husband, and then made a proposal to my manager one month before coming back to work. He agreed to a 50 percent work schedule for the first six months after I returned, and then a 75 percent work schedule after my son's first birthday. With this flexibility, I spend afternoons with our son, mainly outside in the fresh air.

Flexwork can also mean working a certain number of hours from home, sometimes referred to as telecommuting. I was given this option, but after trying it once or twice, I knew I worked best in my office environment and didn't want to bring my work into my home. I opted to simply reduce my hours and keep the hours I do work at the office.

Here are a few things I've learned about flexwork. First, it's easier to make the proposal when you know your manager well and s/he knows your capacity to deliver. Second, for it to succeed, you must be organized, prioritize your workload daily, and avoid taking on more than you can handle. Third, if you succeed with number two, it means you are an amazingly efficient employee! You don't have time to go for endless meetings, coffees, or lunches. Fourth, to prevent office talk like, "She's never here," you should: 1) ask your manager to announce at a staff meeting that you are on flexwork and to state your working hours; 2) let your colleagues know on an ongoing basis what your working hours are; and 3) put it in your professional e-mail signature so people know when they can reach you. I had a satisfying "aha!" moment with a senior manager who was asking a group of us when we were available for a meeting. He turned to me and said, "Before one o'clock, right?" Right!

Formula: For a variety of reasons, you may find yourself in need of formula. I had to make a decision quickly in my eleventh month when my natural supply had run out but my son was still too young for cow's milk. I agonized over the brands, conscious of the debate on additives that are found in many formulas. I ended up going with a German brand, Holle. They have a big range of products, appropriate for different ages. I found a company in Vermont, Organic Start, who was importing from them. You can do easy ordering online, and they deliver in less than two days.

Free Pass: Who doesn't love a free pass once in a while? And quite frankly, who deserves a free pass more than a new parent?! Whether you are the mom or the dad, claim your free passes frequently in those first years and please give them to yourself as much as you do to your partner. Why not even make a game of it—the Free Pass game? For example, when you are sleep deprived and at the end of your rope and snap at your partner, s/he can hold out their hand and offer you an imaginary free pass. I did that a lot mentally in those first months, but what if my husband and I had made it a game between us? We might have broken through the tension of child-rearing a little better and a little faster.

Fund (or Baby Savings): The minute we knew I was pregnant, my husband and I started saving every month from both our incomes in order to fund medical expenses, pre-birth purchases, and post-birth purchases. We opened a savings account with our bank, and I wrote my husband a check every month for my portion. Do whatever works with your financial situation, but please do it. You may well find yourself with a reduced cash flow and a lot of unanticipated expenses during maternity leave.

G

is for . . .

Gas: This is another tricky one like colic, where the causes and remedies are hit or miss. Our little one didn't have gas too frequently, but when he did it was easy to spot because his stomach became stiff like a washboard. My favorite remedy was lying him on his back and doing little circular motions with his legs up toward his belly and back down. This often did the trick; within ten minutes, he was usually passing gas comfortably.

Going Out: In the flurry of new parenthood, it's easy to forget that you are part of a couple. Learning how to go out and leave your baby with someone you trust can be very difficult, but it is essential to focus your attention on your relationship with your partner. Now we have no problem leaving our son with the nanny for a night out of theatre, dinner, or music. We are intentional about planning at least one outing a month as a date night. But in the beginning, it was very hard. The first few times we went out were not pleasant—we quibbled over where to go, or felt deflated (physically or emotionally) when out. But the important thing was that we kept at it. Now we relish the opportunity to put on some beautiful clothes and head out on the town!

Guardianship/Godparents: As difficult as it was, we discussed the issue of guardianship early on. In our culture, godparents assume the role of guardians, so we made our offer to Clyde's prospective godparents with the assumption that they would become the guardian(s) of our son should something happen to my husband and myself. But not all cultures adopt the practice of godparents, and still other don't recognize it legally. So it is important to investigate. One of my dear friends pointed out that in choosing their guardians, they looked for friends who either had children or were child-centered. In her words, it was important that a guardian "can understand what it's like to make decisions for children, and the ups/downs of parenting."

Guilt: As a new parent, there can be a lot to feel guilty about. Breastfeeding, taking time for myself, and going back to work were at the top of my list. And there's no quick fix for any of these issues and the feelings they engender. Despite significant changes in women's roles over the last three decades, cultural norms have not caught up, and neither has our capacity for freeing ourselves from old beliefs and traditions about motherhood. Balancing work with parenting is hard, especially if flexible work cultures are not in place. But our own internal norms around what it means to be an excellent mother also place significant pressure on us to overcompensate when we are home from work.

Several books helped me deal with this during the return-to-work period: *Overwhelmed: Work, Love, and Play When No One Has the Time*, by Brigid Schulte; *The Second Stage*, by Betty Friedan; and *Unfinished Business*, by Anne-Marie Slaughter. Also, a great series of podcasts on the issues around work-life balance, flexwork, and new gender roles at home and in the workplace can be found at the ThirdPath Institute. A central message emphasized in all of these resources is that modern childcare and rearing, in a time when both men and women are in the workforce, is a family issue, not a women's issue. I not only found solace in the experiences of these authors and thought leaders, I also found solutions to problems that my husband and I were facing—problems that, I might add, we were convinced we were facing alone.

H

is for . . .

***Hand-Me-Downs (see also* Op Shop):** Don't be shy about receiving them! Not all of your child's clothing and accessories need to be brand-new, especially when many of the objects will become obsolete quite quickly, given kids' growth rates early on (see *Repurposing*). We received loads of great things from friends—high chairs, playpens, clothes, bottle racks, baby carriers, winter gear. You name it, we willingly accepted it. And when we no longer needed them, we promptly passed them down to other couples who did. It felt so good to regift those objects.

Help: Here is my golden trinity with respect to help: Ask for it. Accept it when offered. Pay for it if you can. Otherwise, you will drown. It could be the simplest thing, like a neighbor of ours who came over one night and offered to clean up the kitchen after dinner. Or our friends who came in the early weeks to see the baby and bring food. I sent people shopping sometimes if they volunteered. These little acts of kindness provide you with crucial time to do other things (like sleep, or do your fifteen minutes of journaling). We didn't have the luxury of grandparents nearby, so after six weeks, when my husband went back to work and was traveling three days at a time, I had someone relieve me for three hours every day so I could shower, go write in the library, go to yoga, meet a girlfriend for a drink and a gab, or just wander the downtown shops and clear my head.

Hemorrhoids: I got them badly from my vaginal delivery. Most hospitals are prepared to help you treat them. It's important to keep up with the treatment when you get home. I did a sitz bath every day for the first three weeks. Every morning, I put a panty liner in my underwear (see *Underwear*) and then lined the panty liner with witch hazel pads. This eased a lot of the inflammation and pain. You also have to be extremely careful not to stress the area, which makes it critical to take a fiber supplement. In my case, I drank a glass of prune juice with one tablespoon of psyllium husk every morning.

Hives (see also Viral Infections): Hives can come as a result of viral infections or being sick, as well as from an allergic reaction. Have your pediatrician take a look before jumping to conclusions.

Honey: Should not be given to a child before the age of one year old.

Hot Flashes: Are not only for menopausal women! Oh my gosh, do I still remember these from my early months of motherhood. They become particularly acute when you are breastfeeding. I tried to always have a Nalgene bottle with icy water by my side when I breastfed to keep my temperature down.

Hydration: This is critical for both you and your baby! Remember that babies don't need any water for the first six months—breast milk is sufficient. But you need to stay really hydrated because breastfeeding drains you of a lot of liquid. As I mentioned above, I kept a big Nalgene bottle filled up and beside me when I was breastfeeding.

I

is for . . .

Image: Once the dust settles (say after nine to twelve months), you might take stock of your closet and treat your year-one motherhood mark with a special spring-cleaning. Your body will go through immense physical changes as a result of your pregnancy, birthing, and then breastfeeding. I got to a point where I was sick of looking at my pregnancy clothes. I yearned for a closet revamp—nothing drastic, just something that signaled, "New me, new life." Plus, everything shrunk in my case (bra, shoes, clothes). I met a wonderful fellow Calgarian, Jamie McClean, who came over to my house, and together we reviewed my closet. We identified clothes that, with a simple tailoring job, I felt I'd love to keep. We put a lot in giveaway bags. And in the process, I became much clearer about clothes going forward. She has a fun little ebook, *#DRESS-CODE*, that helped get me on my way.

Incontinence: Be prepared: your bladder retention will never be the same again. You will find your bladder doing the inconceivable at the most inconvenient times—when you're laughing at a friend's joke, sneezing, or running for the bus. You can't do much in these instances other than cross your legs—if you remember in that split second before. One of my girlfriends has a solution when it comes to running that could be applicable to many situations: wear a thin panty liner. If you're told that this condition will last forever, do not be discouraged. Specialists can fix it, though they recommend waiting until you are sure you are finished having kids. And it is advisable to try physical therapy first (see *Pelvic Floor*).

Instant Illness: Inevitably, you will have a moment when your little one will get sick on a weekend night when the pediatrician's office is closed. Before you rush to the emergency room (which can expose your baby to more illnesses), there are a few other resources to consider. Some pediatricians have a concierge service you can sign up (and pay extra) for that allows you to make late-night calls. Urgent-care facilities may be in your area and have longer hours of operation. The Ask Dr. Sears website has a powerful search engine where you can enter symptoms and get some possible diagnoses and remedies.

Intimacy: Take your time. You may find that your interest in being intimate will be affected by more than simply whether you have physically healed after the birth. Your general energy levels will most likely be low in that first year as you do night feedings and potentially go back to work. You may also experience low self-esteem, as stretching may have altered your body's appearance. Or your hormones may be in flux. If it's not happening, communicate and look for times during the day when you have more energy and the baby is sleeping. But as my husband reminds me, intimacy can be achieved with more than simply sex—for instance, by just taking some quiet time to talk to each other, gauge how you're both feeling, and talking about everything you are both going through.

J

is for . . .

Jammies: It is totally okay and reasonable to leave your baby in pajamas during the day, especially when it is winter and you want to keep them indoors. Don't feel the pressure to get your baby "dressed" every day. Nor should you feel pressured to get up and get "dressed" every day yourself. Yoga pants may well become your best friend in those early days.

Jaundice: Is common with newborns. Our son had it. In most cases, pediatricians will recommend Vitamin D liquid supplements and exposing your baby to low levels of direct sunlight (often through a window). We put our little guy in his car seat on a windowsill in the house for less than ten minutes per day. Normally, with a mild case, jaundice should go away within five to seven days. In extreme cases, phototherapy is required.

***Journal for Baby (see also* Attention):** I wish we had faithfully filled out the beautiful journal my parents gifted us. There are two reasons why: First, for the first few months following Clyde's birth, I'd call up my mom and ask her the "is-it-normal" questions—his weight, when he cut his first tooth, when he ate his first solid, when he took his first step. My mom had no immediate memory of these things, so she'd look them up in my baby journal. Second, even though our son is only two years old now, we have already lost the memory of these "firsts." So when our friends now ask us the same questions, I am at a loss to answer.

Journals can be for more than just "firsts." Another friend of mine took the opportunity to record more than just milestones—she wrote down funny events or moments, or things that were happening in the outside world that she thought her son might find interesting to read when he grew up. Another one set up an e-mail account for her kids and sent them information about their first words or things they did. (This also presents the opportunity to get family and friends to send your little ones their own e-mails about early memories from special occasions like first birthdays or baptisms.) Another girlfriend has now started an art journal to paste in her kids' art from day care. So you can do a lot with journaling!

Judgment: This and guilt are two of the trickiest things you will probably face as a new parent. Parenting and child-rearing often create black-or-white attitudes (see _Parenting Styles_). Women who tend toward people-pleasing will find this tendency toward black-or-white thinking especially challenging. My husband and I have often been unconventional when it comes to the choices we've made for our son. We've found it helpful in the face of questions and raised eyebrows to remember that we are responsible for our lives, not anyone else's. Trusting your instincts will also help you when people raise questions about your decisions (see _Quiet_).

K

is for . . .

Keepsakes: My mother-in-law is the queen of keepsakes. She gave us the bassinet that three generations on my husband's side had slept in, along with a beautiful array of cotton blankets and clothes. Both sets of our parents had also kept several of our toys from when we were young, and these came in handy when visiting. We've now culled a few keepsakes of our own—a knit sweater made by one of my girlfriend's mothers, a handmade wooden-handle hairbrush, and some little boots my parents bought in Spain when Clyde was two months old.

Kellymom.com: For a new parent, the Internet can be your worst enemy. I'd caution against too much surfing on topics of concern because you will inevitably find a barrage of information and advice that, when you're sleep-deprived and overwhelmed, may only increase your anxiety. Kellymom.com, however, is an excellent source for all things lactation and breastfeeding. She smartly curates information, relying on scientific research and evidence to inform readers about specific topics. She was my go-to on all things breast related!

Kindness: It might seem bizarre to have an entry on one of the most basic human values, but you'd be surprised by what can happen between a couple when you are thrown into a completely disorienting life change. Even the smallest acts count. My favorites are the cards my husband left around the house for me—"You Are the Best Mom" in my office tote, or funny animal ones tucked under my pillow. These simple little acts of kindness put a smile on my face and kept me going in the midst of trying times.

When it comes to educating your little one about kindness, it is never too early to start. You can do a lot to communicate through picture books, stories, and even by how you treat plants, bugs, and animals. As my child educator friend reminds me, it is important to teach kindness to your child early on, so that when s/he starts school they have that characteristic in place to use with friends and problem-solving.

Knock-down, Drag-out: I'd like to meet the couple who will not experience one of these fights during the first year of parenthood. When I reflect on our own, it centered around a habit of my husband's that I failed to address with him in the beginning. Instead, I let my irritation build to the point of a complete meltdown. SARK has a really good book that helped me to deal with my own nit-picking, *Succulent Wild Love*. It offers tons of easy, immediate-put-to-use tips on communication, prioritizing issues, and, first and foremost, dealing with your own emotions. I highly recommend it.

L

is for . . .

Labor Coach (or Doula or Midwife): Having extra support is a really good thing when you get to the hospital. Often, if a woman has gotten the help of a labor coach, she may continue with her for the first few months after birth. These trained professionals can be extremely useful in catching signs of post-partum early on and helping their clients to treat it quickly (see *Postpartum Depression*). In the United States, some insurance companies will cover parts of the cost of a doula, but others may not. As a doula friend of mine astutely said, "Submit the claims anyway!" because this is how you build a change movement in the health care system. If enough individuals submit the claims, eventually insurance companies may recognize the demand out there for coverage and adjust their plans accordingly. In the UK, you are automatically assigned a midwife who is also responsible for weekly in-home checkups in the first month postpartum to see how you and your little one are doing, and these services are covered by the National Health Service (woohoo!).

Lactation Consultant: You may have taken a class on breastfeeding prior to giving birth, and perhaps you had a visit or two from a lactation nurse while you were in the hospital (if you gave birth in a hospital). Chances are, though, that when you get home, you are going to run into some difficulties with breastfeeding.

Keep all the reference papers they gave you at the hospital. Try to listen to the lactation nurse at the hospital, even if you are utterly overwhelmed and exhausted. Most of all, when you get home, look up lactation consultants in your local area's health network. They will become your best friends, alongside your partner, masseuse, yoga teacher, and care helper. As described above, breastfeeding is hard! Get support and help. Depending on the state or even the county, lactation consultants are covered under some health insurance plans.

La Leche League: This amazing nonprofit has the simple mission of "helping mothers worldwide to breastfeed through mother-to-mother support, encouragement, information, and education, and to promote a better understanding of breastfeeding as an important element in the healthy development of the baby and mother." They have an excellent website full of resources for new moms. Bookmark it under your favorites!

Life Coach: There are a variety of reasons why a life coach may come in handy once life has settled a bit after childbirth and you are perhaps heading back to work. In our case, we used a life coach early on to help us problem-solve issues. Time management and division of responsibilities were two key issues we kept coming up against, and we didn't feel fully resourced to find the solutions ourselves. Just being able to talk to a third party and discovering that our challenges were similar to those of most new working parents was so helpful. Our life coach provided us with some amazing solutions that we still use today. We specifically chose a life coach that specialized in working couples with young children. ThirdPath Institute has a great roster of life coaches.

Literacy: One of my oldest friends who is also an educator advises that it is never too early to start reading to your child. Even while your baby is still in your tummy, you can start introducing your children to language through books, and to sounds and vocabulary through your speech or songs. As silly as it sounds, just explaining to your little one the basic activities you are doing —"Yes, I am cutting a carrot; this is a knife and this is the carrot"— expands their vocabulary and helps with future language acquisition, literacy skills, and development. Once our baby reached about thirteen months, he showed a lot of curiosity, so telling him about the things we were doing as we went along felt very natural to me. One initiative that caught one of my girlfriends' attention was Too Small to Fail, a public awareness and action campaign to equip parents with the tools to help their kids in early childhood development.

M

is for . . .

Massage: Some of you may have had a prenatal massage in those last weeks when all your limbs were swollen and your back was sore. Postnatal massage is equally valuable in those initial weeks and months after birth. At first, postnatal massage will help to drain fluids from the body and gently reset your system after the trauma of birth. As you begin to breastfeed (or bottle feed) and find yourself holding a little child frequently, your arms and shoulders may become sore, pushing the tension up into your neck. Frequent massages, if you can afford them, can be a useful tool in your self-care toolbox.

When seeking a massage therapist, try to find someone who is specifically qualified in pre- and postnatal massage. The therapist should be familiar with basic comfort issues (like having an appropriate table, and cloths nearby for your leaking breasts!).

Mastitis: This infection comes on swiftly, so you need to be very aware and call your doctor, because it is crippling once it takes hold. You get chills and fever, followed by headaches. At first one small area of your breast may be tender, with a bit of splotchy redness. Later, when full-blown, it will become a hard lump in a localized area. In my case, I was going down for an afternoon nap when I was suddenly so cold I was shivering in bed (despite it being over 90 degrees Fahrenheit outside!). My husband got me into the shower, seated on a plastic garden chair. I took the shower nozzle and held it over the area to get my breasts really warm. Then I used the backside of a comb to massage the blocked area. I did this many times a day.

Even though it's excruciating, the best thing for mastitis is to continue breastfeeding. And to get lots of liquids, antibiotics, and bed rest.

***Maternity Leave (see also* Paternity Leave):** Maternity leave policies in the US are dismally inadequate. Maternity leave—or really, parental leave—is important for establishing parenting norms and roles and for bonding with your baby. Maternity leave is also critical for women's postpartum health.

Despite mounting evidence about its benefits, the US remains the only industrialized nation that does not have paid maternal or paternal leave. I find this shocking, especially since women, according to Pew Research, are the sole breadwinners in 40 percent of families with children in the US.

Research shows a correlation between paid leave and lower attrition rates in the workplace. The US does have the Family Medical Leave Act (FMLA),which allows individuals up to twelve weeks of unpaid leave, but how this is put into practice is left to the discretion of every employer. Thankfully, some states (California, New Jersey, Washington, and Rhode Island) have enacted their own paid parental leave programs, as have some companies, particularly in the tech industry.

Meal Planning (*see also* Help and Visitors): Thankfully, my OB/GYN advised us in advance to stock our freezer with enough prepared meals for one week of dinners. This was one of the most useful pieces of advice we received since immediately following the birth, my husband and I were both exhausted and not interested in cooking or even shopping. In retrospect, we should have planned for more than one week. Depending on where you live, you might also be able to take advantage of delivery services that offer meal planning, like Blue Apron, Plated, or Sun Basket. A Web-based care site such as Care-Calendar is also useful for organizing friends and family who may wish to bring meals to you on certain days.

Metronome: On one of our first nights home, my husband and I were trying to soothe our crying baby. After hours of trying fruitlessly to get him to stop crying, I had to go to bed, and I fell asleep to the wailing of our child. When I woke up for the next feeding and went into his room, I heard a soft knocking, like a ticking clock. There was our baby, sleeping soundly in his bassinet, curled up beside my husband's guitar metronome.

Later that day, I asked my husband where he'd gotten the idea. "From raising puppies," he said. "They want to hear their mother's heartbeat." If my husband has proven one thing time and time again during our early parenting days, it is that he is a resourceful problem solver.

Motherlove More Milk Plus: Make no mistake, this tincture's smell and taste is not appealing. But it could be a life saver if you are struggling to produce enough milk. Put this on your potential support list. Do your own research. Talk to your lactation consultant and pediatrician before taking it.

Muscles (Loss of): After checking with my doctor, I went back to yoga at the six-week postnatal mark. Prior to giving birth, I had practiced consistently three to four times a week for over fifteen years—all the way up until one week before the birth. I was strong and supple.

Nothing could have prepared me for my first class back. I had chosen a beginner class at the local studio. I went to do a modified push-up and couldn't even hold myself up. I could only lie on my back by going on my side first and then lowering down. It was a truly humbling experience. Nothing will prepare you for how much muscle you will lose over the course of your pregnancy. So be gentle on yourself and your body. Be kind and patient.

Six months later, after a consistent three classes a week, I was back to normal. Like all things in life, dedication and determination were key to my recovery.

***Music (see also* Classes):** Live or recorded, our baby loves music! Get out the guitar, piano, rattles, pots, and serving spoons. Whatever the instrument might be, start playing very early on. Kids love rhythm, dancing, and moving their bodies. With any luck, you will too! We signed our son up for a weekly music class when he was six months old and kept him in it until he was two. He loved it.

N

is for . . .

Nanny: I recognize this is a controversial topic, and equally, a privileged one, as not everyone can afford this type of exclusive care. In DC, almost all career couples will have a nanny at some point. The trick is finding one that matches your requirements and your personality, and then navigating the legal requirements for employing one. Nannies are considered employees, and therefore any family hiring one is required to apply for an Employer Identification Number (EIN) with the federal government. Once you receive your EIN, you will be required to file both federal- and state-level taxes for your nanny. Naturally, this means that your nanny must have a Social Security number. Please do these things! Don't encourage people to work illegally in the US, and certainly do not put yourself in a position where you might be caught employing someone illegally. If you don't think you can handle filing yourself, there are payroll companies who specialize in nanny taxes—for instance, HomeWork Solutions, if you are in the DC, Virginia, and Maryland area.

Apart from paying taxes, you may or may not need to offer your nanny certain other benefits, like health insurance, paid sick days, and annual leave. Each state has its own requirements on these issues, so it's best to read up on it. Also, some states now apply minimum wage requirements to all job categories.

We found it useful to draw up a simple contract with our nanny. This was important not only for us as employers but also for her as an employee. (For instance, having a contract allowed her to apply for loans with her bank.)

Nervous System: New moms will experience hormone shifts, and for some of us, this may lead to symptoms like sleeplessness, anxiety, and feeling "revved" or "tired but wired." Dr. Sara Gottfried has some great information on this and how to balance hormones in her book *The Hormone Cure*.

Night Nurses: Are not the exclusive domain of mothers with twins. Even working moms with one child may resort to using a night nurse to combat fatigue (see *Nanny* for a discussion on employing childcare help). In parts of the United States, a night nurse can play a triple function: lactation coach, night nurse, and general helper. I know of some who will gladly come and clean your house or cook a meal. You just need to talk to potential candidates and figure out the breadth of their services. Often, night nurses will have different packages with prices adjusted to reflect the full scope of services you are looking for.

Nighttime Routine: Just like napping and sleeping, routine around bedtime, even in those early months (say after three months) is helpful for everyone. I suspect most people follow the old adage of bathtime, night dressing, a little music, and a bottle or breastfeeding. Some of my friends were even reading to their kids at that point. Whatever it might consist of, the nighttime routine helps baby unwind and get ready to sleep.

Nipple Guards/Shields: One of my dearest friends described these as both a "lifesaver" and a "game changer" when trying to navigate nursing a newborn who wasn't latching properly. Her commitment to breastfeeding exclusively meant finding solutions to the pain and bleeding she experienced when her little one fed. Although I didn't use them, I could imagine how, even if your baby latches just fine, nipple guards or shields could come in handy to prevent everyday wear and tear. I still recall many middle-of-the-night and early-morning episodes hunched over the counter with my nipples in a bowl of warm salt water to soothe the cracks that had developed. It was very painful. My lactation consultant got me on Motherlove nipple cream, which sped up the healing immensely. Another girlfriend swears that Multi-Mam compresses are the best product ever.

Nursing Pads and Bras: Stock up on these two items before you give birth because you will need them almost immediately.

is for . . .

Omega-3s: Coined "brainfood," omega-3s are a great supplement for mom's brain and emotional well-being postpartum. The rich oils ease anxiety and depression symptoms. Omega-3 pills or oil can be easily found in health food stores and in some bigger grocery store chains (see *Postpartum Depression* for more details on doses).

Onesies (with Magnets): You might come to dread diaper changing, not least because of the moment when your fingers just can't quite get those little buttons done up fast enough while your newborn is squirming off the changing table. Fear not: a smart female entrepreneur has heard your cry! In with the magnet onesies, out with the buttons: Magnet Mouse is here. This little innovation in baby wear is a game changer. And yes, she will ship to the US!

Op Shop: Better known in the US as secondhand or consignment stores. These will become a friend to your wallet as your baby quickly grows. I was amazed by all the things you can find there: clothes, shoes, hats, books, toys, strollers, high chairs, etc. We do a quick scour of our neighborhood store every week. If I find something that's a bigger size than we need now, I buy it and keep it tucked away in a closet. Shoes are probably the most coveted item—a pair of brand-new tennis shoes for a one-year-old are over forty dollars. At the op shop? Maybe one dollar, and in excellent shape! Worth fifteen minutes of your time on a weekly basis.

Outside (*see also* Air): Some of my best memories of maternity leave involved a baby, a stroller, and a dog. We'd rise early during those warm summer months. After finishing baby's feeding and changing, then making myself a cup of coffee, we'd be off on one of our town routes. Leesburg has a gorgeous park and trail not far from our house. Sometimes we'd just explore the historic downtown. Where our dog took us was less relevant than just getting out into the sun and fresh air. During those tricky first months of the "witching hour" (see *Witching Hour*), I'd take Clyde out again around 5:00 p.m. and found that helped immensely with settling him down. My husband and I are both big walkers, and the tradition we started with our son at an early age continues now with trail walks. We've gone from jogging strollers to baby carriers to Clyde now walking along on his own two feet!

Overwhelm: Overwhelm inevitably hits every new family. First and foremost, we need to be able to give ourselves permission to be human. There will be moments when everything will come crashing down. The key is to find ways to prevent frequent crashes, namely through self-care (see *Breathing*, *Sleep*, *You*, and *Self-Care*). But moments will come, and in those moments, we really do need to give ourselves permission to feel all we are feeling. A couple of tricks I have learned involve breathing, movement, and journaling. (In her book *Succulent Wild Love*, SARK offers some very simple and amazing journaling techniques to really get at the heart of what you are feeling).

P

is for . . .

Parenting Styles: Do differ, and yours will reveal itself quite quickly after birth (if not before). In all likelihood, you will not even know what style you have until you start muddling through the daily machinations of being a parent. Probably the first test case is bed-sharing (see *Co-sleeping*), followed by approaches to getting your baby to sleep through the night. Depending on where you find yourself on the spectrum, resources abound. One of the really good resources we have used is Dr. Laura Markham's website Aha! Parenting and her book *Peaceful Parent, Happy Kids*. What's great about her website is that she tackles all stages of child development and provides loads of free tips and advice on navigating these major developmental milestones. The most important thing is for you and your partner to be comfortable with the daily decisions that will come your way—sometimes ones that are completely unexpected.

Parents (and In-laws): I gained immense respect for my parents after having our child. Those sleepless nights! That crying! The sacrifices! I will never miss sending Mother's or Father's Day cards again. Many new parents speak of the challenge of establishing boundaries with their parents when it comes to advice on child-rearing. In my case, I was very fortunate. My husband's mother and my mom were (and continue to be) very hands-on when requested but virtually void of any personal judgment. I really enjoyed having them both around during those critical first six months, as both imparted countless old-fashioned tricks of the trade. I also loved watching both interact with our baby and observing their techniques for distracting and engaging with him. They assuaged many of my small fears simply through their relaxed demeanors. Our fathers, too, have been inspirations. It's been a joy to watch everyone be young again!

***Paternity Leave (see also* Maternity Leave):** As mentioned in *Maternity Leave*, there is currently no federally mandated paid parental leave in the US, only the Family Medical Leave Act (FMLA), which allows for up to three months of unpaid leave. Even the FMLA is at the discretion of employers, however, and is only available to companies with fifty employees or more. My husband tried to take parental leave through the FMLA program and discovered just how frustratingly open to interpretation this law is at the company level. The lawyers in his union believed this was leave above and beyond regular vacation time, whereas the company HR department determined that he had to exhaust all his vacation days before FMLA would kick in. In the end, he took two weeks of his vacation leave, but because we had plans to go see our parents in Canada and the northeastern US, we didn't want him to exhaust it all. It was disappointing to see the policy being interpreted in such a fashion, especially when my husband wanted to stay home and care for our baby with me. According to data compiled by the Organisation for Economic Cooperation Development (OECD), thirty-one out of forty-one countries have paid leave earmarked for fathers. The United States is not one of them.

Pediatrician: In an ideal world, you'll spend time finding the right pediatrician for your little one prior to giving birth. In reality, you may not be thinking that far ahead. I was definitely in the latter category. We ended up choosing a pediatrician's office that was near our home and was recommended by friends. But I do know of people who interviewed pediatricians until they found one that aligned with their values. This may be especially important for you if you have less conventional medical views on things like vaccines, natural or homeopathic medicines, and plant-based diets.

Pelvic Floor: Your pelvic floor muscles will become strained during pregnancy and after birth. These muscles are important for a number of functions, but the one you will notice the most after birth is your bladder (see *Incontinence*). As soon as you feel able, you can start to do pelvic floor exercises daily to strengthen this band of muscles. Several websites offer simple routines that can be done while sitting down, breastfeeding, or perhaps at your desk if you go back to work. There are also physical therapies that can be done.

Penaten (see Diaper Rash): This is a little French-Canadian secret. Whenever I am home in Canada or my parents are coming to visit, I stock up. For our son, it has been the most effective diaper rash cream when his symptoms are severe.

Placenta Encapsulation: This has become a more common practice over the last decade in many Western countries, including the United States. Most hospitals in the United States will ask you ahead of time if you want to do placenta encapsulation. There is an additional cost associated with it that may or may not be covered by your insurance, so it is advisable to discuss it with your health insurance provider ahead of time. I did not do it, but several of my closest girlfriends did, and once a doula friend of mine explained the benefits to me, I wished I had too. Apparently, ingesting your baby's dried placenta in the form of capsules is one way to prevent postpartum mood disorders. Older mothers are at a higher risk of postpartum depression, and ingesting the placenta can improve mood regulation.

Plane Games: I hope you will never have to travel long distances with a baby on your own. Should it happen, ask your friends what they use to keep their babies distracted. One of my closest girlfriends gave me this rule of thumb: thirty minutes per game. You calculate the total flight time and work out how many games you will need. On one of my recent trips, it was something ridiculous, like twelve. Obviously, it is not possible to pack twelve games, but I do recommend getting at least five to six under your belt. Pop-up books, sticker books, shakers, and puzzles with big pieces are all great. Avoid anything that can fall on the ground and then roll (little cars, for instance). And as my girlfriend advised, try to make them new objects your child hasn't seen before.

One game that didn't require me bringing anything on board was the "ice transfer" game (my son made it up himself). Take two cups. Get one filled with ice. Transfer it to the other one. Transfer it back. Amazingly, this kept him occupied for thirty minutes. And you get to drink the water as the ice melts. If all else fails and your baby is super fidgety, look to the kindness of strangers . . . that person sitting in the seat beside you.

Playdates: In the beginning, you can't really figure out who these are actually benefiting, you or the baby. Our neighbors have a son about a year older than ours, and we'd have playdates in each other's yard as an excuse to get together for a glass of wine on a warm weekend afternoon. It broke us out of our isolation and gave us a chance to laugh, and to share tons of tips and recommendations. If you don't have many friends with children your age, you could try regularly hanging out at your local playground. In time, you will spot the parent(s) who frequent the playground around the same time as you. You might strike up a conversation and find out that you have something in common. Playgrounds can be an ideal playdate dating ground!

Podcasts: These are great companions when you are breastfeeding. I had a couple of my favorite NPR ones lined up alongside my yoga one (*Tranquility du Jour*). I loved that I could easily stop and start them, depending on how long my little one fed. Especially during those excruciating middle-of-the-night feedings in the beginning, I'd turn one on and just zone out. Now that I am back at work, I relish listening to them during my short commute to and from work. Lately, I've been listening to the ThirdPath Institute's *Thursdays with ThirdPath* podcast—a great resource if you are interested in developing work-life balance habits. And I like *Women at Work*, by Harvard Business Review. It is a series for career women as well.

Postpartum Depression (PPD): PPD can affect both men and women, though rates of PPD are higher in women. PPD can come on as early as pregnancy or as late as one year after childbirth. According to a recent review of clinical studies examining PPD, it usually occurs in the first four to six weeks. Signs include feeling sad, guilty, anxious, irritable, or even angry. What makes these symptoms PPD is their duration—meaning that the symptoms remain for an extended period of time, in some cases up to three years. Given that the symptoms of PPD are also common feelings that any new parents will feel for a short period of time following the birth, it is advisable to speak with your doctor about what you are experiencing and to monitor the length of time you experience the symptoms.

Some natural remedies may help to prevent or treat signs of PPD. A doula friend of mine recommends fish oil to her clients, as it is proven to help in balancing hormones. During pregnancy, you can take regular doses of 3,000 ml/day. Then, following the birth, for a period of no more than five to seven days, you can take a very high dose—up to 9,000 ml/day (see *Omega-3s*). Ashwagandha is another proven natural remedy. I have also heard of friends taking Rescue Remedy, which can be found in most pharmacies and health food stores. Do your own research, and talk to your OB/GYN or your GP before taking anything.

Because the relationship between PPD and stress is proven, finding ways to support your well-being is critical in those early months (see *You* and *Yoga*). For me, yoga has always been an invaluable mood regulator. I suspect that my PPD was rather mild because I was practicing yoga very frequently. If you are a practicing yogi, continuing your practice will help immensely, as will meditation.

Postpartum Health: During your pregnancy, the medical establishment most likely regarded you as little more than a vessel for your little one (that is, unless you sought out a midwife, which, according to the CDC, only 9 percent of American women chose as their primary birth care in 2013). I regret that this is how women are treated, and I regret even more that it really does not improve in the immediate postpartum period, when you need devoted care even more. New mothers experience raging emotions, and I found few outlets for sharing my concerns. While doctors or nurses check on your baby with great frequency after birth (two days, two weeks, one month, two months), your own first visit with your OB/GYN does not take place until six weeks after the birth. I was having problems with my bladder (as every woman who has delivered naturally will), and my stomach muscles felt extremely weak. I mentioned these things, but my OG/BYN didn't say much in response. I understand now that incontinence and muscle loss are common issues, but I didn't know that then because I had no girlfriends with babies whom I could talk to about these things. My OB/GYN probably saw these as common symptoms, but it felt to me like my health concerns were falling on deaf ears.

It is your health, and you have the right to ask and to understand what is going on with your body. There will be such immense changes, some irreversible. Do not be afraid to ask questions and insist that your concerns be heard.

Premature: Babies born prematurely obviously require an extra level of care and support. They will not reach normal development milestones in the same period. What is often forgotten is the extra care and support that parents of preemies need! There is more stress put on the couple and often more trauma experienced by the mother, who will most likely face invasive procedures to deliver the baby. All the regular prescriptions for rest and healing are amplified for new parents in this situation.

Pumping (at Work): There is a reason why so many sensible nations give women a year's maternity leave: pumping at work is d#*n hard, not to mention tedious. All that lugging around of milk, all those pump parts to clean at night, and then having to remember to pack up all the supplies again the next morning. And I was lucky: I went back part-time until I stopped breastfeeding, which meant I only had to pump once at work and didn't need to worry about storing the milk in the fridge there (freshly pumped milk can stay unrefrigerated for up to six hours).

You need good support, resources, and equipment for pumping at work. But you also need to know what to expect. Find out if your office has a lactation room. If so, do you need to get a key or register for access? Will you have access to a refrigerator? Does your employer provide hospital-grade pumps at work so you only have to bring your bottles and parts? If you must bring your own pump, is there a safe storage place for it? Does your insurance cover buying a pump for personal use? (Under Obamacare, most insurance policies did, but check with your insurance company and find out how you can get a pump). You must also consider the pump breaks (typically fifteen to thirty minutes) as part of your work schedule (making sure to block it off in your calendar every day, as you would a regular meeting). And don't be bashful when colleagues ask you why you aren't available for a meeting. We need more education in the workplace about these things.

Q

is for . . .

Question: There is no right way to raise a child. This is perhaps an obvious point, but particularly in the era of the Internet, it can be overwhelming to search for advice on an issue. We found it helpful to identify individuals who we considered "experts" on particular issues—sleep routines, breastfeeding, or feeding, to name but a few. They were "experts" because they appeared knowledgeable but also because they shared our values on the issue. Once we found an expert, we stuck to that person. Some were in-person (lactation consultant), some were on the Web (sleep consultant), and others were in books (dietitian).

Quibbling: It's hard to know where to begin with understanding quibbling. There is the element of personality—of wanting to be in charge—that can make one more dogmatic or even stubborn. There is also the element of sleep loss in the beginning, which makes one prone to being less patient.

As difficult as it might sound, figuring out the root causes of quibbling in your relationship with your partner is important because this type of arguing can persist a lot longer than knock-down, drag-out fights and have more detrimental effects on your relationship. I also think it is especially important to avoid quibbling when it has to do with your baby's well-being and routine because you want your partner to feel empowered to care for your child just as much as you do.

In our case, quibbling most often had to do with routine and what each of us thought was the best way to do things. I learned in the end that it didn't really matter whether Clyde napped at 1:00 p.m. or 1:30 p.m., or whether he was bathed before or after dinner. What mattered most was that my husband felt comfortable caring for our son and establishing his own routines with him.

Quiet: Somewhere along the way between pregnancy and childbirth, most mothers will lose a certain level of self-confidence. It is important to find a way to tap back into your instincts following childbirth, despite the fact that child-rearing seems so daunting and the pace is fast. Resources are readily available, but instincts are what will help you make final decisions you are comfortable with. And instinct thrives in quiet.

My husband was always really good at taking a moment to quiet himself in the face of our wailing baby so he could connect to his instinct on how to act. Quiet is important to cultivate on many levels—not just in the form of a physical space but also in the mind. I often found that even ten seconds of good, solid breathing would reset me when I was at my wits' end.

R

is for . . .

Reading: Few warm feelings match reading to your little one while he or she is sitting on your lap. We went through a period where I read to my son first thing in the morning and then also at night. I had stopped breastfeeding by then, and I found the contact with my son beneficial—a replacement for the loss of our physical bonding post-breastfeeding. As your baby gets a bit older and starts exploring their physical world more, they may shun books for a while. But don't worry, they will come back to them. Just keep them around, and try to keep up with setting aside time for reading, even if brief, in your daily routine.

Regular Checkups (the Importance of): Pediatrician visits can seem tedious and too frequent in the beginning, but it is so important to stick with them. This is where monitoring of developmental milestones occurs, where vaccines will be administered, and where general questions and concerns you have will be addressed. It is also where you can be screened for postpartum depression (see *Postpartum Depression*). If possible, you should identify a pediatrician ahead of your child's birth, possibly by asking your friends who have had children. Try to make sure it is within a reasonable distance from your house since you will go frequently in those first few months.

Repurposing: You will cycle through, sometimes at a gallop, a lot of specific baby items and find yourself feeling guilty as you contemplate throwing them away only a few months later. Burping towels? We use them as washcloths. Bottles? We take them on walks in the forest and put little stones and acorns in them to carry home. Breastfeeding covers? Perfect blankets for the warm summer nights. Pants too short? Make them into cut-offs for the summer. The list can go on. Be creative!

Research: It is difficult these days to feel secure in the decisions you make for your child. Information abounds on the Internet. Advice from colleagues, fellow parents, and neighbors is plentiful. Sometimes what everyone else is doing just seems like the easiest way to go, even if in your heart you feel otherwise. Perhaps being a social scientist has made me approach decision-making with intention. I've gotten plenty of books out of the library, observed other parents and their interactions with their little ones, and then made my own decisions with my husband about our parenting style. This has been the right way to go for us. Having an inquisitive mind as a new parent will pay off, as child-rearing challenges increase with age.

Routine: Every culture approaches this issue differently. Where women fill the primary childcare role and also must make an economic living, a discussion on routine is a luxury. I understand this from having worked and lived in many countries in sub-Saharan Africa, where small babies ride on their mothers' backs to mines, fields, and trading posts. But here in North America, routine is a big topic of conversation. My experience proved the importance of routine in nurturing a calm baby and ensuring sane parents. An old friend from South America remarked on this once when visiting. At 5:30 p.m., I said I had to excuse myself because it was time to get my son ready for bed. My friend was surprised: "This early?!" Her own kids, ages two and four, didn't go to bed before 11:00 p.m. and still slept in her bed. She admitted that she had never created a routine with them, and that this was coming back to haunt her as they grew older.

I can understand why parents shy away from routine early on. You have already suffered the complete loss of your independence. When those waking hours start to stretch out longer, you have an urge to break free, to do things on your own time. But when I think about what a good sleeper my little one is, I know it is in part because he had a good routine from an early age. That doesn't mean running your baby's life on a clock, but it does mean staying aware of the time in between waking, feeding, and sleeping, and keeping to a regular rhythm. Some really great books that kick-started our routine choices included *Secrets of the Baby Whisperer,* by Tracy Hogg, and *The No-Cry Sleep Solution,* by Elizabeth Pantley. Weebeedreaming.com also has a great sample schedule for establishing nap and sleep routines as of three months of age.

S

is for . . .

Self-Care (see also You): This may seem like an obvious necessity, but mothers get caught up in a lot in the beginning and forget to take care of themselves—in part because time simply does not seem to be on your side, but also because you feel this need to be present in every moment. I really liked listening to the *Tranquility du Jour* podcast episode where Kimberly Wilson spoke with Sheila Pai, in which Pai evoked the image of *mindful self-care*. Two key points in this: First, move slowly and consciously through your self-care practices. Breathe them in. Rejoice in them. Do not rush through self-care as an exercise to tick off the list, e.g., "Yoga: done. Massage: done." Second, self-care does not need to involve money. It can be as simple and free as walking. Or sipping a delicious cup of coffee in your living room while enjoying the silence as your baby naps. Or relishing in a bubble bath. These are all simple, luxurious self-care practices you can incorporate into your day.

***Skin-to-Skin Contact (see also* Touch):** This is strongly recommended immediately after birth. The benefit of skin-to-skin contact (SSC) doesn't stop there; we are encouraged to do it as often as possible, for as long as possible. Even vulnerable babies are brought out of their incubators so that SSC can work its magic. A senior London midwife who has delivered over a thousand babies describes it beautifully as the "womb on the outside." Just a few of the wonderful and vital effects of skin-to-skin contact include lowered stress levels (cortisol) in mother and baby, better milk production, quicker initiation of breastfeeding, temperature and heartbeat regulation, natural pain relief, and the transfer of the mother's friendly bacteria, providing protection against infection. The additional emotional and psychological benefits cannot be overestimated. Babies' neural development and sense of security, and the bonding effect on parents, is profoundly impacted by SSC.

Sleep: It's important to grab naps whenever you can in those first months after your baby is born. Accept every offer you receive from someone you trust to look after your little one so that you can rest. Establish a very clear routine with your partner around night and morning responsibilities so you both get adequate sleep. It is critical for your own well-being, and for your relationship.

Sleep Sack: Imagine a sleeping bag worn like a shirt. We used different ones in all the seasons (weebeedreaming.com has a great guide for using differently weighted sacks for different temperatures). We even had one that was the weight of a Canadian sleeping bag that we used when our son was five months old and we vacationed in the Rocky Mountains. I really liked the HALO brand— the fabric has a slight stretch, and they offer tons of options in weighted fabrics. Although some sacks can be worn up until two years old, we found that sleeping sacks only worked for Clyde until he was about one year old.

Soothers (aka Binkies): Our son never took to one, but he loves his thumb! The only time I really wish he had taken up the soother was in that period after we stopped breastfeeding but before he understood instructions and we were flying in planes. His ears would get blocked and he'd be cranky, but I couldn't explain to him how to yawn, suck his thumb, etc. Nowadays there are so many cool soothers, including one for boys with a mustache on it.

Stroller (*see also* Travel System): If obsession is ever a virtue, it is in the hunt for the perfect stroller. It is up there in importance with finding the perfect diaper since in all likelihood you will use your stroller for several years. All the rage at the time of my son's birth was the "travel system"—the handy concept that you could put your little one in a car seat, click it onto a stroller, and transport him or her around that way, and, when need be, transfer the car seat into the car seat base. But not so fast! Once you've settled on travel system or no travel system, you've got to face the plethora of choice.

Having some criteria in mind helps. Ours were pretty straightforward: 1) rugged tires so we could walk in fields and on grass; 2) lightweight; and 3) durable (so it would last more than just a year or two). This brought our choice down to two options: Thule or BOB. During our last getaway before Clyde's birth, my husband and I decided to hit the REI to try out our two options. Funny how after all our research and agonizing about specs, we were suckers for a good deal: the travel system for BOB was on sale. We never looked back. It has been the most brilliant stroller for us—wading through muck at horse shows, slogging through muddy fields, rolling over plenty of tree roots and branches on walking trails, and performing effortlessly on urban sidewalks.

Swimming: We took our son into the community pool at just three months old. It was amazing to see how comfortable he was in the water, allowing us to float him on his back or his tummy. Then we stopped for a good nine months. Curiously, when we started going to the pool again, it was difficult to get him to let us move him around as we had when he was younger—perhaps because he had developed a keener sense of awareness by then—and he clung to our necks in the water. In retrospect, if we had kept up with regular exposure to water, it might have been different. My advice would be to keep at it from a very young age. It doesn't need to be for long periods of time—twenty to thirty minutes is ample.

T

is for . . .

Tax Credits: Federal legislation allows parents to claim a tax credit of up to $3,000 per annum (for one child) to cover certain childcare expenses. In my husband's case, he also benefits from an employer-based program that allows him to put in a certain amount of money before taxes every year to cover childcare expenses. This is called a Flexible Spending Account. It is worth investigating to see if your or your partner's company has a similar scheme.

Teething: Can manifest itself very differently from child to child. Our son had a runny nose and a slight temperature, combined with the need to chew on everything. We had been given Sophie at our baby shower, and she certainly came in handy. We didn't try any of the soothing balms that some pharmacies carry, nor did we use the amber necklace. One of our good friends used it, however, and she swears it reduced her son's teething pains.

Time: The first time someone tells you how fast children grow up, it sounds so cliché. But after having gone through two-plus years of it, I get it. Time does go by fast, and most of it goes unrecorded. The other day, someone asked me when our son got his first tooth and when he first walked. Sheepishly, I told them I honestly couldn't remember. My husband continues to be so good at capturing time with his camera—he takes plenty of photos and videos. In the first year we did a nice album for our loved ones using Shutterfly. But then life got in the way.

Time also means being in the moment, of course (see *Attention*). Both my husband and I try on a daily basis to remind ourselves to be fully present with our son, playing and engaging with him with no cell phones or other distractions on hand. In her book *Peaceful Parent, Happy Kids*, Dr. Markham proposes a nice way to do this with her "fifteen-minute games."

Touch: My husband's experience with raising puppies was put to use at a very early age with our baby. We spent an enormous amount of time holding our baby and encouraging our family members and close friends to do the same. Doing so provides babies with a sense of security and allows them to develop strong bonds with their caregivers.

Travel System (*see also* Stroller): The only disadvantage I found with a travel system was how heavy the combined weight of the car seat and our baby was once he got a bit older. He was on the big side, and lifting him up and down in the seat was hard on my back. Other than that, I would definitely recommend a travel system.

Travel Tips (Air): Don't be that parent we take pity on in the airport. You know, the one who is running between gates with a baby on their hip, pushing a stroller, and hunched over with an overloaded diaper bag. A lot of stress with air travel can be avoided with some thoughtful planning. For one, give yourself *ample connection time:* if you have an international connecting flight, give yourself at least two hours to get through immigration, pick up and recheck your bags, and go through security on the domestic side. Strive to be a *minimalist traveler*: try to get your laptop and other carry-on items into your baby's diaper bag. Carry only a small travel purse for yourself. Avoid strollers and go with a baby carrier instead. Save yourself from *the hassle of security checks:* wear comfortable shoes that you can slip on and off for security. Do not pack liquids! *Research required legal documents*: for international travel without your partner, make sure you have a notarized letter from them authorizing you to travel with your child outside the US.

U

is for ...

Unconditional Love: Being a parent has taught me what unconditional love really means. It is a gift to experience this with your child. Now that Clyde is a bit older, I've found myself meditating on this from a different vantage point: how to extend the concept of unconditional love to others—both those I know and those I don't know. Meditations abound on this subject, but some that I have found particularly useful and inspiring can be found on the Insight Timer app. I stumbled recently upon the practice of *tonglen*. It is a Tibetan meditation practice based on the idea of giving and receiving. I am hooked!

Understanding (What's Happening to You and Your Baby): Every mother's experience is different following childbirth. Some experience highs and lows; others may not. Some will get hot flashes; others will not. Don't be shy about speaking with your general practitioner or asking fellow mothers if they have experienced symptoms like your own. If you have specific websites that you trust, consult those too. For instance, when I found my milk supply reducing to practically zero, I immediately reached out to my lactation consultant and read up on the research at Kellymom.com. Within twenty-four hours I had a new game plan to get me through the last month of breastfeeding before I could transition little Clyde onto cow's milk.

Underwear: If you are reading this before you have given birth, please do not be alarmed. You are going to experience bleeding for at least a couple of weeks after delivery. As with other undergarment investments (see *Nursing Pads and Bras*), you are going to want to buy new, inexpensive underwear that you will have no guilt over throwing away when the time comes. I went for good old Hanes, and I bought them one size up from my pre-baby size. I made sure I had plenty of pairs tucked in my dresser prior to my birth date. (PS: Switching out your underwear once your bleeding stops for your pre-baby ones may have the added effect of rekindling your physical relationship with your partner.)

University Fees: In the US, there are a few investment vehicles made available to parents and extended family members to save for university expenses. The most popular is the 529 college savings plan, but others include Education Savings Accounts (ESAs) and custodial accounts. Speak to someone at your bank or look them up online, as each one differs in its advantages. Try to set aside a small sum for university every month after your child is born through one of these vehicles. Some states also offer incentives for parents to save for their children's university education.

V

is for ...

Vaccines: Our pediatrician's office was good about telling us in advance what vaccines we could expect our child to get at each upcoming visit. However, nurses don't always inform you that you can split the vaccines to reduce how many side effects your infant experiences at once. We asked for this alternative schedule. Instead of having four or six shots at one visit, we scheduled half the first time, and the other half two weeks later. It meant more visits, but we felt more comfortable doing this for our son. It is important for every parent to be informed and make their own decisions regarding vaccines. It is also important to be knowledgeable about your school district's vaccine requirements and the corresponding exemption process for sending your child to day care and school unvaccinated. For example, in New York

State you can file for a vaccine exemption under religious grounds, but the process is cumbersome.

Vagina: My husband and I still joke about the one instruction that stood out for us from birthing class. Our instructor took us through three hours of visuals and discussion about the physical changes and impacts pregnancy has on the female body. We had just finished reviewing the actual birthing process, replete with a video, when she told us, "Now remember, folks, nothing in the vagina for six weeks. I mean nothing!" I don't know how many times my husband and I laughed about that once we were home with Clyde.

Viral Infections (*see also* Hives): These can cause skin rashes, acne, or hives. It is always good to consult your pediatrician before panicking. One of my girlfriends recommended this great book, *If Your Kid Eats This Book, Everything Will Still Be Okay,* by Lara Zibners, which helped assuage many of her day-to-day worries about minor health-related matters.

Visitors (Managing Them): Visitors are a catch-22 in those first weeks. You are exhausted and overwhelmed, so having people visit can be very useful. On the other hand, some visitors may prove to be more work than you can handle. Establishing ground rules is crucial. If you feel it is important for you, you can set up a calendar and let people know the days and times that you will receive visitors. You could also ask all visitors to bring something practical instead of gifts and flowers (see *Meal Planning*). Depending on how you are feeling, you might also let people know that you will not be hosting them (e.g., serving coffee or snacks). If visitors are very close to you and you feel comfortable doing so, you could ask them ahead of time if they would help you with something like laundry or vacuuming or cleaning the kitchen (see *Help*). Don't be shy! Also, let people know that if they are sick they should refrain from visiting until they are fully recovered.

Visual Electronic Media: Just say no! Your little one does not need any screen time yet. In fact, the American Academy of Pediatrics recommends that children under the age of two not watch ANY TV or videos. And this includes baby app games! Ironically, Silicon Valley parents who developed cell phones and tablets are now banning their nannies from allowing their small children any screen time. See the full *New York Times* article on this, "A Dark Consensus About Screens and Kids Begins to Emerge in Silicon Valley," and read the comments after it; they contain amazing tips for parents with young kids on how to ban, or at least limit time on, devices.

W

is for . . .

Walking (see also **Outside and Air**)**:** As soon as you feel able, walking hits all the right spots for your well-being and your baby's. But take it slowly at first. I remember my first walk, three weeks after delivery, to the local library. With baby in tow, I set off at my pre-baby pace. I regretted it. Even though the library is normally only a seven-minute walk from our house, it took me double that time, and I came home with minor spotting and cramps.

After that first library venture, I introduced small increases into my walking routine every day until after about another month, when I felt more or less back to normal. Having a dog certainly helped, especially when my husband went back to work after the first six weeks. Every morning when he was away, I woke up with Clyde and got him ready because Murphy, our dog, needed a good walk almost immediately. I put my baby in the stroller and off we went for about forty-five minutes to an hour. Many of my fondest memories of maternity leave are of those early-morning walks in the spring and early summer. The rolling hills of northern Virginia formed the backdrop of our tranquil outings as we followed the simple route around our town. Sometimes we'd stop for a few quiet minutes on one of the many benches that line the pathway. Other times we soldiered on as fast as we could, given the rapidly rising temperatures and humidity. Murphy forced me to get out more than I otherwise would have chosen to. I am eternally grateful to him for that.

Weebeedreaming.com: Who would have thought that a sleep consultant in Grande Prairie, Alberta would become my go-to for sleeping advice? This website is an absolute godsend: very straightforward, and designed as a series of blogs that roll between most of the more pressing questions we have as new parents. I especially appreciated her twelve-month sleep routine calendar, which outlined a typical day in the life for babies at every month's interval.

White Noise: Along with blackout curtains, this is one tool in the sleep toolbox that really works. There are plenty of "white noise" machines and apps, though we didn't use one. Instead, we used two household items that provided a dual function: a fan and a humidifier. Ultimately, it doesn't really matter where the noise is coming from, as long as it is there, constant, and preferably loud.

Witching Hour: Once your baby starts lengthening their awake time between naps, the last few hours before bedtime become a messy dance with lots of fussy behavior. Your baby may seem unsettled no matter what you do. This was a super tricky issue for us from about month one to three, although it may be longer or shorter for others. Movement helped a lot. Our house has an open kitchen with an island in the middle. We'd roll Clyde around it in the stroller to occupy him while we cooked dinner. At about five or so most evenings, I would go on a short walk to settle the baby. Then my husband would take over. He has the most amazing reserve of patience. He'd play all kinds of goofy games with the baby on his lap, or play him the guitar. Whatever it took!

X

is for . . .

Xtreme: In those early days of motherhood, every emotion is heightened. As with many of the earlier entries on managing specific feelings, I found some simple techniques quite useful, like breathing and making time for myself. Most importantly, I appreciated this advice: allow yourself to live in these extremities without judgment.

Y

is for . . .

Yoga: "Is it really possible that I have no stomach muscles left?" This thought kept racing through my head during my first yoga class after giving birth. I had waited over six weeks before signing up for a class entitled "Basics." Though I had been an advanced student prior to my pregnancy, I was being utterly realistic about the journey my body had been on since then. The most important thing is to forget what you think you were before childbirth and be gentle with yourself. For three months, I immersed myself in "Basics," "Yin," and "Flow 1" classes. I literally had to reteach my muscles (and ultimately, my brain) how to do sun salutations. I had lost almost all my stomach muscles, my legs were wobbly, I had little attention span, and my arms were feeble. I was lucky that I could go three days a week. After about six months, however, I noticed considerable improvements. If you cannot get someone to care for your baby while you take a class, look for "baby and me" yoga classes targeted to women after giving birth. It may not be totally suited to your needs, but a yoga class gets you out and has the advantage of possibly introducing you to other like-minded new mothers. If going to a class is just not possible, there are plenty of videos online or audio recordings that you could do at home if you can find a moment. Beyond the physical benefits of yoga, focused breathing is shown to improve concentration and reduce stress, two laudable goals to achieve as a new mom.

You (*see also* Self-Care): Pace yourself. Parenthood is a long road. While it is natural to put yourself out there for your baby all the time, with time you will burn out. It is especially hard as a mother, for most women struggle to put themselves first (see *Guilt*). Everyone else's needs trump yours, and then there are the annoying tasks of keeping the house semi-clean, or whatever other day-to-day "to-dos" haunt your lists. Whether it is your *fifteen minutes of journaling* or *yoga* or a *massage* or a *glass of wine with a girlfriend*, it is important to take those small moments. Not only does this give you some much-needed breathing space, it also helps you to reconnect with another, equally important part of you: the pre-mommy you.

Z

is for . . .

***Z's (see also* Sleep):** As every mother has told their daughter when they have a baby, make sure to nap when your little one naps! You will need all the Z's you can get. As tempting as it is to do other things in the first months when your baby sleeps, the most important thing you can do for your health and sanity is to sleep.

Zipper: This came in handy as a little game when our son was learning to use his hands and develop coordination (roughly eighteen months old). Go to your local sewing store, or go online, and buy a zipper that has extremely large teeth (like for a duffel bag). Hand it to your child. He or she will play around with putting the two ends together, pulling it up, pulling it down, and taking it apart. We'd take it in the car on road trips, or just have it hanging around the house.

AFTERWORD

When I embarked on this writing project three years ago, I had a few scribbles in a journal. The urging to turn my few little tips and tricks into a book came from my husband, Clyde, and my good friend Jocelyn. What I had thought would be a small exercise in putting pen to paper quickly grew in ambition—and with that came the support of many friends and family members.

The most significant, unintended consequence of this project has been its cathartic effect. Through the writing, I processed many messy emotions. I thought back to what I would have done differently (or better) and made note of where potential to change, or still do better, was possible. This is important to consider because one of the most striking lessons I have learned in these first three years of motherhood is that although there are so many myths surrounding child-rearing, it is the hidden social norms, especially for women, that trump us up as new parents. Unless we take a step back and think about why we react or make decisions as we do for our children, we risk reflexively repeating old parenting habits or imitating current social norms just for the sake of it. I hope these tips will inspire you to chart your own course, knowing there is no single, right way to raise a child.

A big thanks to the following people who believed in this book from the beginning: Patricia Millar, Dr. Jocelyn Kelly, Dr. Catherine Hynes, Fiona Jager, Rachel Mills, Kate La Rue, Jamie McClean, and my parents, Patricia Bond and William Perks. A special thanks to Professor Sherry Linkon, who did one of the earliest read-throughs and edits of the manuscript and gave me the two thumbs-up to keep at it. A big thanks to Dani Shapiro, who gave me the lead on a publisher when I was discouraged and ready to throw in the towel. And I am grateful to Bridget Boland, who is not only an amazing editor but also a true writing coach. I would not have gone the final distance without you. And of course, last but not least, a tremendous thank-you to my husband, Clyde. Thank you for all your support and encouragement, and all the laughs over these years. My journey as a mother and a professional would not be possible if I did not have a partner like you—someone who views my ambitions and desires as equal to yours.

RESOURCES

APPS:

Insight Timer: www.insighttimer.com
Sprout: www.sprout-apps.com

BOOKS:

On child health:
If Your Kid Eats This Book, Everything Will Still Be Okay, by Lara Zibners

On eating:
First Bite, by Bee Wilson
Stress-Free Feeding, by Lucy Cooke and Laura Webber

On parenting:
Peaceful Parent, Happy Kids, by Dr. Laura Markham

On relationships and love:
Succulent Wild Love, by SARK and Dr. John Waddell

On returning to work and work-life balance:
Overwhelmed: Work, Love, and Play When No One Has the Time, by Brigid Schulte
The Second Stage, by Betty Friedan
Unfinished Business, by Anne-Marie Slaughter

On sleeping:
The No-Cry Sleep Solution, by Elizabeth Pantley
Secrets of the Baby Whisperer, by Tracy Hogg

On women's health:
The Hormone Cure, by Dr. Sara Gottfried

BREAST CARE:
Motherlove More Milk Plus: www.motherlove.com

Motherlove nipple cream: www.motherlove.com
Multi-Mam pads: www.multi-mam.com

BREASTFEEDING AND FEEDING ACCESSORIES:
Boon Grass countertop bottle drying rack: https://tomy.com/
Brest Friend: www.mybrestfriend.com
Dr. Brown's bottles: www.drbrownsbaby.com
Munchkin bottle brush: www.munchkin.com
Organic Start: www.organicstart.com

BUM CREAMS:
A&D Ointment: https://www.webmd.com/drugs/2/drug-92880/vitamin-a-and-d-topical/details
Combat-Ready Balm: www.skincando.com
Penaten: https://www.penaten.ca/en/baby/penaten-original-medicated-cream.html

MEAL DELIVERY COMPANIES:

Blue Apron: www.blueapron.com

Plated: www.plated.com

Sun Basket: www.sunbasket.com

MIRACLE BABY APPAREL:

HALO SleepSack: www.halosleep.com

Magnet Mouse onesies: www.magnetmouse.co.uk

MOBILITY:

BOB stroller: www.bobgear.com

Boppy Tummy Time Pillow: www.boppy.com

Ergobaby Adapt Cool Air Mesh baby carrier: www.ergobaby.com

NANNY TAXES:

HomeWork Solutions: www.homeworksolutions.com

PODCASTS:

ThirdPath Institute: www.thirdpath.org
Tranquility du Jour: www.kimberlywilson.com
Women at Work: https://hbr.org/2018/01/podcast-women-at-work

TEETHING:

Sophie: https://sophiethegiraffe-usa.com

WEBSITES:

Aha! Parenting: www.ahaparenting.com
American Academy of Pediatrics: www.aap.org
Ask Dr. Sears: www.askdrsears.com
CareCalendar: www.carecalendar.org
Jamie McClean: www.ambitiousimage.com
Kellymom: www.kellymom.com
La Leche League: www.llli.org
Shutterfly: www.shutterfly.com

ThirdPath Institute: www.thirdpath.org
Too Small to Fail literacy campaign: www.toosmall.org
Wee Bee Dreaming: www.weebeedreaming.com

ABOUT THE AUTHOR

Following over a decade of working and living in sub-Saharan Africa, Rachel Perks moved to Washington DC in 2012. Shortly thereafter, she met her husband at a horse race in Virginia, at which point the biggest adventure of her life began: motherhood. Though her professional career has brought her to war zones and developing countries across the globe, motherhood has proven to be by far the riskiest yet most rewarding assignment she's ever accepted. *The Little A to Z* is her response to the frequent feelings of overwhelm, isolation, and confusion she experienced as a foreigner navigating the early days of parenting in the nation's capitol.

Author photo © Jonathan Davidar

She Writes Press is an independent publishing company founded to serve women writers everywhere. Visit us at www.shewritespress.com.

The Self-Care Solution: A Modern Mother's Must-Have Guide to Health and Well-Being by Julie Burton. $16.95, 978-1-63152-068-6. Full of essential physical, emotional and relational self-care tools—and based on research by the author that includes a survey of hundreds of moms—this book is a life raft for moms who often feel like they are drowning in the sea of motherhood.

The Doctor and The Stork: A Memoir of Modern Medical Babymaking by K.K. Goldberg. $16.95, 978-1-63152-830-9. A mother's compelling story of her post-IVF, high-risk pregnancy with twins—the very definition of a modern medical babymaking experience.

Braided: A Journey of a Thousand Challahs by Beth Ricanati, MD. $16.95, 978-1-631524-41-7. What if you could bake bread once a week, every week?

What if the smell of fresh bread could turn your house into a home? And what if the act of making the bread—mixing and kneading, watching and waiting—could heal your heartache and your emptiness, your sense of being overwhelmed? It can. And this book will show you how.

Happier At Work by Gayle van Gils. $16.95, 978-1631522048. Practical applications of mindfulness and compassion, along with inspiring stories of companies who apply these principles, for the more than 70 percent of people in US workplaces who are disengaged and stressed.

Note to Self: A Seven-Step Path to Gratitude and Growth by Laurie Buchanan. $16.95, 978-1-63152-113-3. Transforming intention into action, *Note to Self* equips you to shed your baggage, bridging the gap between where you are and where you want to be—body, mind, and spirit—and empowering you to step into joy-filled living *now*!